SHRAPNEL

SHRAPNEL

poems by

George MacBeth

Macmillan

© George MacBeth 1973

SBN Boards 333 14136 9
SBN Paper   333 14137 7

First published 1973 by
MACMILLAN LONDON LIMITED
London and Basingstoke
Associated companies in New York Toronto
Dublin Melbourne Johannesburg and Madras

FOREWORD

When I was a child, I used to walk in the streets of Sheffield collecting shrapnel after an air raid. Those twisted, scorched, rusty scraps of metal were from bombs and shells. They were cold, shapeless things in themselves, the remains of a gigantic jig-saw of violence and pain. These poems are the shrapnel from what explodes in the nerves, or seems to, when people are at war.

ACKNOWLEDGEMENTS

Some of these poems have appeared, or will shortly appear, in the following magazines and anthologies, to whose editors my acknowledgements are due: *Acorn*, *Ambit*, *Crabgrass*, *Isis*, *Lines 12*, *The Listener*, *The London Magazine*, *The Little Word Machine*, *The Malahat Review*, *The New Statesman*, *The Photographic Journal*, *The Poetry Review*, *Stand*, *The Trans-Gravity Newsletter*, *Young Winter's Tales*.

CONTENTS

I

LOVE PRAYERS

October 1970

I

TO THE MISTRESS OF THE NIGHT SEA, THE LADY DOLPHIN

Lady dolphin, barometer
of fortune, moving
through broken lead of the sea
          towards what new absolutes

I have no heed of,
concede me, I pray you,
that I, in all sincere need,
          should ask your guidance

towards my true love,
as others once
asked and were granted
          your guidance to heaven.

II

TO THE SUN, WHO IS A RIVER OF HONEY

Knowing you as now
        that which

you would claim
        to be always,

I mean
        a particular blessing,

betwixt the steel
        of sinks,

unlocked refrigerators,
        and

the blind fire
        in the stale wall

that bleeds for me,
        O sweet sun,

be a juice of dark joy
        here,

this hard breakfast-time,
        in the contours

of missing her,
        of losing everything.

III

TO THE MASTER OF THIS BOOK, THE LORD GORILLA

Sire, be merciful,
    be merciful
    to the bare white multitudes
    who lie still
in the cauldron of London,

of whom I am one,
    who have abused you,
    and forgive them,
    and comfort me,
as I lie here crying.

IV

TO THE LIONS OF THE NIGHT, ANGELIC PRESENCES

Lions, angelic presences
        in the furnace
of Regent's Park,
        I say, rise,

lords of the saw-dust,
        from your fallen glory
in the cat-cage
        to a new sand-height,

beautiful
        as the mane of Asia
on the neck
        of the sea,

I mean that
        continent
of the dream you
        mount, hunt, in

where I am a child,
        at ease now
knowing you
        are awake all night long

with claws bared
        as close as the key
in the door, dark lions,
        lion-masks in a ring.

V

TO THE SMALL CREATURES OF THE DARK

Out of the dark
into the red moon-light of the corridor,

out of the dark
into the artificial day of your cages,

out of the dark
howling,

out of the dark
for the sake of new food,

in your mottled skin,
gathering hair, wool, and scales,

wings pleated,
or at ease in a straw nest,

so many of you,
believers in what the light will do,

and fearing it,
all fall, creep, run and prey,

all rise, flap, sing,
all cry to teach me,

I beseech you,
out of the dark,

into the dark
of another day,

all fly, step, waver,
all reach, leap, wander,

all come,
all bow down,

all pray for me.

VI

TO THE FLY, LIGHT OF TUESDAY

Fly, on
    the dry glass, in
    your black
    noise, rake

of oblivion, that
    beats through
    this mild Tuesday
    where the sparrow-song

is oblique to
    my easy
    breakfast, my
    egg and

marmalade, O
    small fly,
    still
    on the dry glass,

be a rich
    nuisance now, be
    a virulence and an
    ecstasy

to the ingrown
    bedevilled
    soul-nail
    of my self-love.

VII

TO THE MASTER OF ALL DECEITFULNESS, MY LORD SPIDER

Lord spider,
who walk always
        in
the toils of a dark
        ingenuity,

I pray, sire,
be a bright anxiety
        of singleness
this night, and teach
        the webs

of my strange liking
to shape themselves
        more easily
to the patterns of what
        is for her, a proper love.

VIII

TO THE LORD SHARK, WHO IS A MYSTERY IN DARKNESS

O Lord shark, if she should fall,
                    before I do,
towards that silence
wherein blood is shed
below the sea of the dream,
                    I ask your violence,
implacable as it must be,

not to be sore on her, nor falter
                    against her enemies,
knowing how many times
there has to be something
still dying
                    to meet what needs food,
and is always open, shifting between the little fish.

IX

TO THE SPECK, WHO WAS A LIFTED FURY

O fierce, clutched
    thing, stiffener,

as she would be,
    sickened,

or saying so,
    by such tricks,

have pity,
    have pity,

on all who would
    evacuate

your eminence
    from their coarse vicinity

towards the corridor,
    and the cold.

X

TO THE SISTER OF TWILIGHT, THE MISTRESS PRIMROSE

Lady of coolness,
        magnificence
        incumbent
on a high stem,
        decider
of what the sun will do,
if not tomorrow

then today,
        sister of twilight,
        lemon
before the salt
        of the fish-grey
we call dark,
I mean, the night,

swallow, I ask
        in all
        calm,
into the deep throat
        of your being,
uncurled for the long
draught of moon-sweetness,

whatever is sick
        and longs
        for purpose,
whatever may need renewal,
        whatever
steeps itself in the brine
of belonging,

knowing only
          the need
          seeping
through all its pores
          for a lost
loved thing, lying
apart, and alone.

XI

TO THE CREATURES OF LEATHER, IN WHOSE PRESENCE I REST

Lords, by whom I am surrounded,
      vested in ruin,
still before the slight intensities of
      the small hours,

lords, in whose intelligence of sound
      I am remembered,
resting in moving silence,
      or lost in dreaming, at ease

after so much toil in the manufacture
      of forgetfulness,
and until whatever dense effort
      the morning may demand of me

in November, as it will be,
      I pray be in all things
my aid, my example, and my refreshment,
      certain as ever,

lords, creatures of crow's feet in the eye corners,
      of what you are,
and of where your skins will be,
      before her, and after me, and for ever.

XII

TO THE INHERITORS OF THE DARK, MYSELF AND ALL

Out of the clock's ticking,
        into rain
        hissing,

out of the bed's creaking,
        bodies
        turning

before each other's light, I
        cry
        strike,

fail, be abnormal, creatures
        of whom I am
        one,

lying all round the lived earth
        hoping
        for a dawn

without red heat
        along
        the brain dying,

flying
        into the never-closing wound
        of tomorrow.

XIII

TO THE MOLE, WHO IS A SHADOW OF NOTHINGNESS

Mole, if you are there,
      as I believe you to be,
      generous as velvet
over the ungloved fingers
of the slow-worms,
      who die in trying,

as all must,
      wherever there seems a chance,
      to rise
into the sun,
be a secret sharer
      with us, I pray you,

of all you own,
      master of neat
      foot-steps
in the corridors
of rhizomes,
      incurable roots

in strain already
      for the next Spring,
      I mean that year
growing to my face
tight as mould
      eager to feel its way in,

as you would,
      to her place of sorrows,
      moist as moss
against your little hands
groping,
      that I touch and kiss.

XIV

TO MY CAT, WHO WAS SICK IN THE DARK

Lord, even the small being,
as you are,
        subjected to the limits
of endurance,

exposed in the grey places
of the night,
        where all is uneasy
as the sea's turning

over and over,
be free now, be
        an exposition
of deliverance,

an enormous
violent relief
        before the windows
of wherever we live,

shadowy lovers,
completed and hopeless,
        anxiety flying
through our eyes open

for ever and for ever
towards
        a blank strangeness
that comes and comes.

II

LADY SYCORAX

A LITANY

Creature of barns
in your mask,
lord of the grass of Madagascar,
colour of soot
in Minahassa
or New Britain,
lord of the common grass
in Celebes,

  tyto, invoco te

Master of the bay,
the bay of the Congo,

  phodilus, invoco te

Who screechest in common
or in the tropics,
with your belly of a lion,
white throat
and black cap,
creature of worms who screechest,
of whiskers and spots,
who screechest in the Pacific
in your beard
and dark crown,
or in Puerto Rico,
bare-legged,
becoming red,
or in flames,
lord of the common called Scops
in your collar
and strange markings,
in Andaman
with your white front
becoming red

19

in Biak
and Flores,
thou who art now a rajah
in Celebes
or lesser Sunda,
who art my Mentaur
and lover of cinnamon,
lord who art called the giant
of Madagascar
with your white face,

   otus, invoco te

your mane,

   jubula, invoco te

and crest,

   lophostrix, invoco te

lord of the great horns,
who art an eagle,
an eagle with spots,
creature of the Cape,
loving milk
and known to Fraser,
to Akun
and Shelley,
lord of Malaya
and of the Philippines,
of the forest
and of the twilight,

   bubo, invoco te

20

master of fish in Malaya,
of brown fish
and of the fish the colour of a lion,
the fish of Blakiston,

    ketupa, invoco te

lord who art fishing for worms,
known to Pels,
becoming red

    scotopelia, invoco te

in your spectacles
barred with rust,
and your white chin,

    pulsatrix, invoco te

lord of the snow

    nyctea, invoco te

and the hawks,

    surnia, invoco te

creature of iron who art a pigmy,
a pigmy of the North,
smallest thing in the world,
in the Andes
or in Cuba,
creature of Europe and Asia
with your red chest
and chestnut back,
lord of the jungle

who art marked with pearls
and barred,
in your collar,
with the voice of a cuckoo

glaucidium, invoco te

or an elf,

micrathene, invoco te

lord of the hawks of New Guinea

uroglaux, invoco te

who barkest
in Boobook,
as the Great Hawk,
becoming red,
in New Britain
and the Admiralty Islands,
creature of speckled hawk-flesh,
lord of Molucca
with your back of soot
in the Solomon Islands
or in New Ireland,
with your ochre belly of a hawk
as in the Orient,
in Andaman
or in the Philippines
or as a hawk in Madagascar,

ninox, invoco te

creature of bare legs,

gymnoglaux, invoco te

who art laughing

sceloglaux, invoco te

because you are small
and with spots,
with spots in the forest,

athene, invoco te

lord who art burrowing

speotyto, invoco te

and mottled,
black and white,
or with black bands
becoming red
in the wood of Africa,

ciccaba, invoco te

lord who art barred
in Brazil,
with legs becoming red
and with spots
in Lapland,
or as a lion
in the Urals,
know to Hume as a lion
or in the brown wood
mottled
and with spots, in the wood,

strix, invoco te

creature of stripes

rhinoptynx, invoco te

and long ears,
lord of the Styx
and of Abyssinia,
and of Madagascar,
with your short ears
in the African marshes,

   asio, invoco te

lord of Jamaica,

   pseudoscops, invoco te

who art fearful,

   nesasio, invoco te

sharp as a saw,
as a saw turning without spots,
and with your buff front,
lord of the farthest North we have ever known,

   aegolius, invoco te

tyto,
phodilus,
otus,
jubula,
lophostrix,
bubo,

24

ketupa,
scotopelia,
pulsatrix,
nyctea,
surnia,
glaucidium,
micrathene,
uroglaux,
ninox,
gymnoglaux,
sceloglaux,
athene,
speotyto,
ciccaba,
strix,
rhinoptynx,
asio,
pseudoscops,
nesasio,
aegolius, ora pro nobis

LADY SYCORAX

In the wings
   of a dragonfly,
   I see you,

In the carapace
   of a beetle,
   I touch you,

In the words eating
   out of my hand,
   I taste you,

In the sea casting
   skeletons,
   I smell you,

In the death-watch
   ticking,
   I hear you.

A HYMN

praise to
what is
existing
beyond
through all
our time to come

in the morning
rising
before I do
still
dreaming
of what to praise
in you
that is what you are

in the evening
fallen
within the circle
of the girdle
of bone
around
what it is
you rise from

possessing
whatever
it is
you enter
breaking
through
or without
opposition

sure
of a welcome

wherever
you come
now
and tomorrow

knowing
all things
eager
to rise
as you do
and believing
they will

to what opens
in all
times
and places
ready
to receive them

> *praise to*
> *what is*
> *existing*
> *beyond*
> *through all*
> *our time to come*

28

A SPELL

hérisson, hérisson

Word for a pig, word for a sow,
word for an ugly old woman,

word for the point of a spear,
word for a thorn,
word for a harrow,

ireçon, ireçon

hiding in sheaves of corn,
     in bales of hay,
hiding in rushes cut for thatching,

pitched into a wagon,
     crossing the sea on faggots to Amrun,
stranded on floating logs,
     on floating islands of turf,

Algerian,
     with a bald patch,
long-eared,
     between the Casplan and the Sea of Azov,
with a narrow skull in the steppe and the desert,
     or in the gorges of the Balkans,

riccio, riccio

Word for a pig, word for a sow,
word for an ugly old woman,

word for the point of a spear,
word for a thorn,
word for a harrow,

ireçon, ireçon

feeding on worms,
      on wood-lice,
feeding on apples and fungi,
      on eggs of the corn-crake,

living in small caves,
      in the burrows of shelldrakes,
living in cracks in the rocks,
      in hollow tree-trunks,
living in walls of dry stone,
      in the under-floor spaces of barns,
living in arched roots,
      in tangled old heather,
      in thatched reeds,

erizo, erizo

Word for a pig, word for a sow,
Word for an ugly old woman,

word for the point of a spear,
word for a thorn,
word for a harrow,

ireçon, ireçon

hérisson,
ireçon,
riccio,
erizo, veni,

in nomine erinacei primi, veni

III

THE SOIL KINGS

I

THE LESSER HORNED ARTICHOKE

This rare and
captured
one squats
in a sieve,

hissing. It
marshals
its host
of peaked leaves, wanting

to bring
something to birth. It
hatches a
plan, spits

froth of
a buttery
stew
in

a pan. It
makes its name,
dies,
and is eaten, leaf by leaf, to the bone.

II

THE MALE SEA ASPARAGUS

In its
eternal
search
for a mate, the

male
sea asparagus
advances
with all its appendages. It

finds
its glaucous
love
subdued

in a heart-white
napkin,
nude
before

the ravages
of the sea. It
enters
her sighing.

THE SPIDER-HUNTING AUBERGINE

After dark,
with the shepherd's-crook
of its antennae
out, this gloomy predator

stalks through
the dusky glades.
There,
knitting its orbs,

all unawares,
the great leviathan
of the silk-works
is lurking.

One touch
of those poisonous
mandibles
and that furry arachnid

is a goner.
Then
that gross aubergine
lays its eggs in her belly.

IV

THE MASKED AVOCADO

It is
a poor ball
or function that is not graced
by the masked

avocado,
cane,
skin, and *vinaigrette*.
Through both

of its black eyes
this gay seducer
cons
the midnight world

of the sea-bed
or the dance-floor.
Extending
a bark-like claw

from the sands of time,
it sucks,
most elegantly,
a little dry, enclosed air in.

V

THE SHORT-TOED RUNNER-BEAN

In its green
winkle-pickers, this
inconspicuous
creature

fades
without a
sound
into the dusk. At

midnight
when the elves
are
foraging, and

trees creep
into
their own
shadows, you

sometimes see
one
eviscerating
a pair of transfixed nail-clippers.

VI

THE CRAB-EATING BEETROOT

With its raw
maw, and
vertiginous
appetite

for lung-worms, you
would scarcely
credit how
many

small crustacean items
it can
pack away, this
haunter

of the ice-floes,
immaculate
as a red whale.
All things

with claws avoid it.
In a good season,
we sometimes
harpoon one with a scythe.

VII

THE FALSE CABBAGE

There is only
one
way to prove
the false cabbage.

Place
your reluctant visitor
on the back
of a clean envelope,

extract
one ounce
of green blood
from

its tail
or hindquarters, and
suck
the offending substance

into your
nostrils.
If it be false,
a noxious fume will swell forth.

VIII

THE NORTH AMERICAN WHOOPING CARROT

It sounds
off at the most unexpected
moments. Just
when you think it might be time

for lunch, it
sweats out
its protest. Far away
in the mountains of somewhere

like Utah, you
hear it whooping it up
with the Swedes,
very loudly.

I dare say
it *is* rare, but
I don't hold
with all that:

oink oink
it says, though,
like a man with a bad cough,
repeating himself.

IX

THE TRUE CAULIFLOWER

Others
may seem to be
it, but the
true

variety wears
its heart
on its sleeve.
Leafing

through an old
bed
of bean-shoots,
or a cabbage-plot,

you might
come on one,
white
and a little shaken,

with its
ear
to the ground,
hearing no evil.

X

THE LITTLE BROWN CELERY

As it wanders
through
the grisly forests
of the kitchen-garden,

the little brown
celery
is accustomed
to sing:

*Three bare
patches in
the cabbage-bed.
Three bare*

*caterpillars
learning to
fly.
Cabbage-white,*

*cabbage-white,
soar in the sky.
I shall be a salad
before I die.*

XI

THE GREAT CRESTED CUCUMBER

It runs
to a chill,
baize
crescent, as

sharp
as
a claymore in
the dry flesh

of sandwiches. It
evicts
dead
butter, bread

rolls, dodging
the webbed
fingers
of the vicar's wife

at garden-parties. It
roams,
unsliceably deranged,
through the bean-rows.

XII

THE PIGMY SPERM LEEK

If you cut
one open, it
screams,
yielding

a black pus
before
knife or
vagina. Vicious

in captive
solitude, it
yanks
its hair out

of the ground,
bewailed
by the Israelites.
Tainting

the breath, it
remembers
the crime of Onan, spilling
its own seed.

XIII

THE SLOW LETTUCE

It goes
on one hinged leaf
over the soil,
shoe-horning itself

into
whatever
plots it
finds vacant. It

spends
a dry
week on its bed,
sluggishly. It

evaluates the
perforated
spaces of its
own abdomen

as if
about to begin
a most catholic sentence. Its
last word is *prey*.

XIV

THE VAMPIRE MARROW

If ever
you walk
after dark
in

the quieter parts
of
your own
intestines, watch

out
for the inky, tar-like
excrement
of the vampire

marrow. It
snores
all day
in a hole, stretching

only
at midnight,
with its wings beating,
for a bite to eat.

XV

THE HAMMER-HEADED MUSHROOM

It swims
in its own
oil,
arcs

along the rock
shelves
of the hind mind. It
spouts

a voluminous
white water,
dying
into the

failed light
of
an Arctic
solitude. It

spins
its melon-slice of
a mouth, inhaling
a scent of leaves.

XVI

THE DEATH WATCH ONION

As if at a wake,
it weeps
in the ceiling, wears
mourning hues

in its layered
hair, as
its bleak young
hatch and

fly. Be
not fooled by
such
behaviour. Its

black
jaws are already
at work
in your drawers. That

cracking
that you hear
is
their broken hearts.

XVII

THE HOODED PARSNIP

It stoops
through
the wet forests
of Ayrshire, as

white and
vulnerable
as an old woman. At
the witching-hour

it snouts
earth
up
from the bottom

of a stiff
mound, rumpling
its
ashen hair as

it aches
into
a sitting position
near to the moon.

XVIII

THE BOTTLE-NOSED PEA

It flaunts
a bulge
in its forehead, owns
intelligence

like
a cyst of corrupt water. It
rolls,
boiled,

through the glass
waves
of jars, bruising
its nose. Emitting

a
gluttinous
and oily
wax, it

becomes
hated, hunted. Then
it explodes,
blubbering, in a scalding lash of fluked light.

XIX

THE SOLITARY PEPPER

It goes
alone over the
blasted heath,
sneezing. Its

rugged
face confronts
ill winds that
bode

nobody good, as
it licks
dandelions
bare

of pollen, wanders
into
the purlieus
of the sallow

catkins, asks
only
for a little bit of bread
and no cheese.

XX

THE PYRENEAN MOUNTAIN POTATO

All winter,
sick
on the dry
smell of brandy, it

soils
its own furrow
with
a hot manure. But

when
the sun explodes
from dust
in

the fresh summer, it
splays
broad feet
over

new ground,
horny,
white-furred, and
sweet as iron on the tongue.

XXI

THE HOLLOW-FACED RADISH

It moans
like a lantern
swinging
in fog, roots

through old
rubbish-dumps
for a bone. When
it hears

the cramp of dust-bins
closing, it
screws
those leathery filaments

in
its ears to
their blank crunch,
scavenging.

It grows
on the backs of
mole-skulls,
depositing vermin.

XXII

THE CREAM LONG-HAIR TOMATO

For all
the
rotundity
of its thick

sides, this
light herb
assails
heights of the glass-house

with
a pursed lip. It
climbs with
a sort of swollen,

glacial
disdain, running
to
seed. It sheds light, hiding

in the graceful
veils
of a beady-eyed
frogs-spawn.

XXIII

THE GIANT WOOLLY TURNIP

All year
it lurks
in the turf,
thick

as a bomb. But
at Halloween,
uprooted,
randy,

it gropes out
by lantern-light
of its own
bowels,

yowling
for food. With
a sweating
mob

of hot Swedes, it
stumbles
into a bonfire, crackling,
and is burnt alive.

XXIV

THE PALE CLOUDED YELLOW-WATER-CRESS

It
breaks
from a chrysalis
of lips, is

a film
of
gauze on
the black

sponge
disintegrating
in shell-holes. It
breathes a scent of mustard. In

all
the seven hours it
flies
before

salting
its grave
in the bean-row, it
never winces, lies, or empties its lungs of blood.

IV

WAR POEMS

THE SIRENS

I grope for time
In its precise cold place.
Violence is bright
Behind my hollow eyes
That milk the war for rhyme.
That sound is lies
I say began each night

And was the one
Remembered by the few
Tied to the mast
Who lived. I hear it grate
Against the April sun,
Then separate
As fragments, and blow past.

THE WAR

I seem to hear,
In those bombed houses where
I echoed in
The empty rooms,
An air

As if, in their
Consumed expanses, what
Was there before
This living chill
Is not

A smell of rot
Only, and mouldered wood,
But something more
Like an old skin
That could,

If someone would
Renew its odour, smack
Of warmth, and life,
And what consumes,
For lack

Of fuel, crack
As timber, or as mines,
Hushed, like that one
Whose early fall
Refines

All that my lines
Here and before contain,
And makes them burn
Into a grief
Again.

THE PASSING ONES

They do not die.
Moved to another shelf,
They lie in shadow. Where
The bombers fly

To burn Cologne,
Rain drenches the cold air.
I wake, and ask myself,
Hearing their drone

And echo, where
My father is, whose death
Was thirty years ago.
I halt them there,

Beating the sky
Into the mould of bread.
Their pilots live. Their breath
Injures me. Why

Do those I know
Retire into blank snow
And freeze there, as if dead?
The minutes flow

Into a bowl
Where people scald, and flare
Like tapers. In my bed
I sense the whole

Burial of parts,
Rib, liver, guts and brain.
I know the worm, the crow
Gagging at hearts,

At lights, at end
Of all we were, and are.
I threaten what has fled.
    I call my friends

Out of the soil
And from the funeral jar
To come in blood again,
    I hear, in oil

And petrol, one
Remembered scrap-iron car
Start where its owner bled
    And someone gun

The two-stroke, sure
Of where he has to head,
North to the border. Far
    Behind him, pure

As cream, or snow,
A woman with a hat
Settles to grief and pain.
    All that, I know,

I may say here
In Germany, on a train,
Writing through dark like tar,
    Must seem from fear

That I shall lie
As they both do in earth.
I say what I have said:
    They do not die.

Turning, they try
To hide from other birth
And be, as when first wed,
    Withdrawn to a high

    Moment, on shelves
Above the meat of things,
Where they can dream, and wait,
    And be themselves.

THE DYING CALF

So rising late
That Saturday, we drove towards the sea,
Tired from our show. And having parked the car,
Walked in a dream of caring, past the slate
And shale of Westbay. There, below the cliff,

Half-caked with mud,
A calf had fallen. Shivering, it lay
Like broken driftwood, near the tideline. If
The air had feathers for the cold, some should
Have settled there. On stones of unconcern

The seaborn light
Watered a space wherein the body spread
Its final claim, to make our footsteps turn
And be Samaritan. As others might,
If they believed, we thought that it would live,

And so walked back,
And telephoned a vet, and waited there,
Four caring ones. One talked. One tried to give
Some thought to verse. One laid his anorak
Along its back. I watched the muddy hide

As it pulsed, pulsed. So
When the police came, and carried it away
Still living, in a sack, I felt no pride
Or stupid hope. Its death seemed long ago,
Stripping all muscle from the bones of verse

And making love
Like we had shown dishonest, Pausing, as
The sun came out of clouds, I felt the curse,
Placed like a falcon on our brows, above
And near the eyes, the curse of caring, pass

And stoop to ground
Along the sand. Across the sea, far out
I saw the light fall, turning, with no sound
Over and over, as we talked about
Our poetry, and die along the grass.

POEM BEFORE BIRTH

Rising from bed
I shaved. Outside, the birds awoke
And sang in pleasure through the rising mist
With bells and cars. Then something turned and spoke
Inside my borrowed head
These words that follow, and were found. Light kissed

The ploughland, white
With naked scythes. If it was Love,
Or what I wanted to believe was that,
I hardly knew then. But in air, above
The sparrow's broken flight,
Returning from his nightlong hunt, the cat

Saw the fine day
And mewed for joy. I heard, and shared
His bleat of praise. As others rose, and made
The old wood flustered, as if it, too, cared
Throughout your house, I say
I never knew how far Love was obeyed.

The clock's low snore
Resounded in its brazen frame
To help the time. The wind made fastened leaves
Turn in the larches. And the cherished flame
That fell in ash before
The gathering of darkness, clasped in sheaves

Like wheat. The chair
I sat in seemed to flower, and snow
To roses with a scent. Inside my throat
The wine of our good meal began to slow
And wake to vineyards. Bare
In my new body's fort, I touched the moat

Round my content
And felt in love. So I wrote out
At peace, and for my pleasure, these few words
To thank my evening host. Here, never doubt,
    I have to say, in scent
Of burning pine, to touch the air with birds,

        Joy comes. Today
So honoured by the care of friends
I rise to feel safe. And when time begins
And nothing but the emptying cellar ends
    With breakfast, and the way
Towards another room, life moves on fins

        In water, child
Swimming to birth. So I, who praise
My lodging in a doctor's house, approve
Ceremonies of beneficence. That blaze
    Along your windows, wild
As what went hunting all night long, was Love.

THE BROKEN ONES

Today I hear
Through troubled iron of my own concerns
Of how his are. He speaks, as always, in
That strangled candour, and my whole world burns
As he announces marriage. I begin

Through violent air
To dwindle from his days. Outside, black rain
Slants across London. An Alsatian runs
To and fro past his penthouse. And again
I crush my papers, wishing they were guns

And we at war
With someone. Years away, in Furness Fields,
I see boys running, buttered by the mud,
At war with Westbourne. One boy scores, one yields
A face of stiffened longing. Where we stood

At school, in time,
The years are melting. Others are in tune
Along the naked wires. The broken places
Focus and die. A boy is beaten. Soon
Stripes in the cheeks will fade, the burning traces

Alter and fail.
I mount the rostrum, anguished in my grace
To read the lesson, furnish them with souls.
Power never known. All falter in the race,
Thrashed down like fish. Set breathless into bowls,

Glassed from our world,
The great sea rising, we become that sperm
I feel one summon, prick out, in a shed.
The death's-head lifts another like a worm
Outside the Gardens, and that power is dead

Wherein we lived
In fettered honour. On this telephone
I live again my childhood, the soaked head
Raging against maturity, the bone
White from my father's body, never shed

Save as long tears
Gliding along the window. Whirled, and lost,
The past goes tortured into earth, and spoils,
Foundering, and useless. On my skin, embossed,
I bear the medals of those burning oils

Torn from a shell
And severing his future. By the wall
There in the kitchen, still delivered, she
I stride out and open in all women, tall
And flat before death's onslaught, mothers me

With love I hate,
Spit back, and spurn. So in this office, dressed
In cured skin from a world I want to share,
I watch a dog run barking, held and blessed
By his master's caring. And I turn to prayer,

Not for myself,
Though that has been, but for my closest friend,
The polio-torn, the brave one. Cracked and spewed
From the world's belly, that will never mend,
I ask the blood-shot to let up their feud

For a short space
And honour him, as I. May he and his
Through casts of measured silence and true sound
Flourish and never sicken. May his alliance
Bleed into glory from far underground

And rise in sons
To blaze for ever in the night of shells
That bred us in the North. May he in joy
Walk through the morning to the chant of bells
And wake in marriage. May no power destroy

That healing love
I see, and fall from. Turning to the flame
That seems to burn for ever in my head,
I settle from his changing, still the same,
Loving the broken ones, the never dead.